Let God Help You Choose Your Husband

"He Will Pick A Winner Every time"

*"And the rib, which the LORD God had taken from man, made he a woman, and **brought her unto the man**." Genesis 2:22*

Dexter & Petula Jones

UWriteit Publishing Company
Goldsboro, NC USA
www.uwriteitpublishingcompany.com
www.soulmatesolutions.org

Let God Help You Choose Your Husband by Dexter & Petula Jones
Copyright © 2012 by Dexter & Petula Jones

ISBN: ISBN-13: **978-0615621746** (UWriteIt Publishing
Company)
ISBN-10: **0615621740**

First Printing April – 2012

Unless otherwise indicated, Scripture quotations in this
book are from the King James Version of the Bible.

This publication is designed to provide information in
regard to the subject matter covered. It is published with
the understanding that the authors are not engaged in
rendering legal counsel or other professional services. If
legal advice or other professional advice is required, the
services of a professional person should be sought.

Printed in the U.S.A.

Dedication

We dedicate this book to our Lord and Savior Jesus Christ who is the head of our lives. We dedicate this book to our heavenly Father for blessing us with a marriage that is truly ordained from heaven, a God given relationship between Soul Mates. We dedicate this book to our children Brandon and Jasmine, you are the seeds of the righteous, and therefore we know that God shall bless you both in life with the mate of your souls.

TABLE OF CONTENTS

Introduction

Introduction

In order to get the most out of this book, here are some questions as you begin this journey of allowing God to help you choose your husband. The first set of questions is, "*Do you know what kind of man you should marry? Is it the kind of man that God says you should marry according to the scriptures or is it just a figment of your imagination of a man?*" The next set of questions is, "*Is that man you are with appointed by God for you? Are you 100% sure that he is the one or do thoughts of doubt and uncertainty arise in your mind at this question?*" Well you better know with one 100% accuracy and undeniable faith or you had better walk away from that relationship and seek the will of God for your life.

1

The Man That God Appoints

"And the rib, which the LORD God had taken from man, made he a woman, and brought her unto the man." Genesis 2:22

You don't have to take risk with your heart when God has anointed and appointed a soul mate for you. The scripture says, *"It is not good that the man should be alone; I will make him an help meet for him."* Genesis 2:18 God has appointed a person for your life that is designed especially for you. The fact of the matter is that *"No other person can do for you what your soul mate can do for you."*

Your soul mate is equipped to love you, cherish you and help enable you to be the best person that you can possibly be. Man without woman is not a good thing, neither is woman without man. Everything that God created and made in the first six days of creation He said it was good or very good. Only in the statement concerning man being alone that He said something was not good. Genesis 2:18 The reason that this incident was not good is because man needed woman to aid and supply him with that which he cannot supply himself. God saw that man needed a companion to be like him but opposite of him. Someone that would complement him and correspond to him equally on his level, yet be his opposite and be a help meet to him. Woman needs man as much as man needs woman. The real true need of **both individuals is** companionship, **and this** is a spiritual and soul need that the man supplies to the woman and the woman supplies to the man. There is an ideal woman for every man and an ideal man for every woman. Man needs woman because woman supplies to him that which no other creature can. Woman needs man because man supplies to her that which no other creature can.

We will show you why these two individuals need each other and exactly what they supply to each other.

MAN/WOMAN WOMAN/MAN

"It is not good that the man should be alone; I will make him a help meet for him." Genesis 2:18

Spiritual = Mankind is a spiritual creature made in the image and likeness of God. Because mankind is spiritual their ultimate and first heart cry is to be connected with their creator God who is also Spirit. Mankind is a tri-fold being consisting of spirit, soul and body; each part of mankind needs to be connected with a being greater or equivalent to him/her. Mankind's second heart cry is to be with someone equivalent yet opposite of him/her. God's ideal plan for mankind is for them to be joined together with an individual of the opposite sex in marriage and be one. *"Therefore shall a man leave his father and mother, and cleave unto his wife: and they shall be one flesh."* Genesis 2:4 However, God doesn't want you to just join up with anyone, He wants you to be joined with your Soul Mate and life mate. This spiritual connection and oneness can only be experienced with someone of the opposite sex. *"And the rib, which the LORD God had taken from man, made he **a woman**, and brought her unto the man. And Adam said, This is now bone of my bones, and flesh of my flesh: she shall be called Woman, because she was taken out of Man."* Genesis 2:22-23

Physical = Mankind also has a physical body and within his physical makeup God has put in him/her a desire to be intimate with one equivalent yet opposite to themselves. The scripture says, *"Male and female created he them. And God blessed them, and God said unto them, Be fruitful, and multiply, and replenish the earth."* *Genesis 1:27-28a* The only union that God blesses is a union between a male and female. A union between a male and male and female and female is abomination in the eyes of God, *"Thou shalt not lie with mankind, as with womankind: it is abomination. If a man also lie with mankind, as he lieth with a woman, both of them have committed an abomination."* *Leviticus 18:22, 20:13 "For this cause God gave them up unto vile affections: for even their women did change the natural use into that which is against nature: And likewise also the men, leaving the natural use of the woman, burned in their lust one toward another; men with men working that which is unseemly, and receiving in themselves that recompence of their error which was meet. And even as they did not like to retain God in their knowledge, God gave them over to a reprobate mind, to do those things which are not convenient."* *Romans 1:26-28* Man with man or woman with woman are not appointed to be Soul Mates with each other. The only appointed Soul Mates by God are male and female. Within this appointed union God has put a holy desire to be with each other physically in an intimate and sexual manner and He has remedied this by way of marriage in order to satisfy this longing and passion saying, *"Nevertheless, to avoid fornication, let every man have his own wife, and let every woman have her own husband. I say therefore to the unmarried and widows, It is good for them if they abide even as I, But if they cannot contain, let them marry: (the remedy) for it is better to marry than to burn."* 1 Corinthians 7:2,8-9

Mental/Soul = Mankind also needs communication and intellectual stimulation with his opposite. Man and woman are mentally wired different and man needs woman and woman needs man to balance the communication and intellectual stimulation of one another. Mankind cannot get this balance from one like himself or from any other creature. When man/woman deprives themselves of woman/man they short circuit their makeup and will never be all that God has designed for them to be. The Bible says the relationship of man and woman *"is a great mystery"* but it's a mystery that God honours, anoints and appoints. Also, there is a fellowship and relationship that mankind need with his/her opposite that creates a social connection that also fill a void which cannot be filled by any other means. Man needs woman and woman needs man and to deprive the two of each other will cause them to *"become vain in their imaginations, and their foolish heart will become darkened." Romans 1:21b*

Sisters, God Will Bring You to the Man

Many times we have had a wrong interpretation and understanding of the scriptures and our lack of understanding can cause us to be destroyed. How many times have you heard *"Sister, the man will find you don't you worry about it?"* I heard one sister that have been single for over 25 years say, *"well it seem like that man has lost his way he needs to get on track."* God has never told the man to find the woman we have misinterpreted the scripture that says, *"he that findeth a wife findeth a good thing."* We will talk about the truth of this scripture in our sister book address to the man, **"Let God Help You Choose Your Wife,"** but for now let's explain why God will bring you to the man.

As a woman of God you are so precious, unique and priceless and God has set it up through his divine wisdom to make it easy for you. Throughout the scriptures we see that God has always brought the woman to the man not the man to the woman. This first begin in the book of Genesis, here we see that after having created Adam God stated that *"it is not good that the man be alone; I will make him an help meet for man. And the LORD God caused a deep sleep to fall upon Adam, and he slept: and he took one of the ribs, and closed up the flesh instead thereof; And the rib, which the LORD God had taken from man, made he a woman,* **and brought her unto the man.***"* *Genesis 2: 18, 21-22*

God brought Eve to Adam he did not bring Adam to Eve. No man of himself is wise and intelligent enough to find a virtuous woman, only God knows and can find a virtuous woman and then God anoints her and appoints her for the man and brings her to the man.

Through his omniscience wisdom he orchestrates the whole scenario and set it up so that the woman will run into or come across the man in some form or fashion. It's not up to the woman to figure out how this will happen, it's her job to believe it and conceive it into her spirit and then it will manifest as surely as the night follows the day. Do you still need more proof? Many times we hear women saying they want their Boaz, but the story of Ruth and Boaz is one of God orchestrating a scenario with the purpose of bringing Ruth to Boaz not Boaz to Ruth. Here is the story, *"Now it came to pass in the days when the judges ruled, that there was a famine in the land. And a certain man of Bethlehemjudah went to sojourn in the country of Moab, he, and his wife, and his two sons. And the name of the man was Elimelech, and the name of his wife Naomi, and the name of his two sons Mahlon and Chilion, Ephrathites of Bethlehemjudah. And they came into the country of Moab, and continued there. And Elimelech Naomi's husband died; and she was left, and her two sons.*

And they took them wives of the women of Moab; the name of the one was Orpah, and the name of the other Ruth: and they dwelled there about ten years. And Mahlon and Chilion died also both of them; and the woman was left of her two sons and her husband. Then she arose with her daughters in law, that she might return from the country of Moab: for she had heard in the country of Moab how that the LORD had visited his people in giving them bread.

Wherefore she went forth out of the place where she was, and her two daughters in law with her; and they went on the way to return unto the land of Judah. And Naomi said unto her two daughters in law, Go, return each to her mother's house: the LORD deal kindly with you, as ye have dealt with the dead, and with me. The LORD grant you that ye may find rest, each of you in the house of her husband. Then she kissed them; and they lifted up their voice, and wept. And they said unto her, Surely we will return with thee unto thy people. And Naomi said, Turn again, my daughters: why will ye go with me? are there yet any more sons in my womb, that they may be your husbands?

Turn again, my daughters, go your way; for I am too old to have an husband. If I should say, I have hope, if I should have an husband also to night, and should also bear sons; Would ye tarry for them till they were grown? would ye stay for them from having husbands? nay, my daughters; for it grieveth me much for your sakes that the hand of the LORD is gone out against me. And they lifted up their voice, and wept again: and Orpah kissed her mother in law; but Ruth clave unto her. And she said, Behold, thy sister in law is gone back unto her people, and unto her gods: return thou after thy sister in law." Ruth 1:1-15

As you can see in this story, Ruth was in the city of Moab and Boaz was in Bethlehem, as we stated earlier God did not bring Boaz to Moab to find Ruth but he brought Ruth to Bethlehem to her husband Boaz. Do you need more?

In the case of Isaac and Rebekah the story is told in this manner, *"And Abraham was old, and well stricken in age: and the LORD had blessed Abraham in all things. And Abraham said unto his eldest servant of his house, that ruled over all that he had, Put, I pray thee, thy hand under my thigh: And I will make thee swear by the LORD, the God of heaven, and the God of the earth, that thou shalt not take a wife unto my son of the daughters of the Canaanites, among whom I dwell: But thou shalt go unto my country, and to my kindred, and take a wife unto my son Isaac." Genesis 24:1-4*

Abraham servant was sent to Mesopotamia, unto the city of Nahor to find a wife for his son Isaac. Genesis 24:10 Isaac did not go with him to find his wife but the servant went there to bring his wife to him. This is the way God does it and when you allow God to help you choose your husband then He will appoint that man for you by bringing you to him, then you will not make a mistake in choosing a spouse.

- Sisters, you don't have to go looking for a man.

- You don't have to run behind no man.

- You don't have to go up to no man and give him your number and tell him to call you and make the first move.

- God will make the first move by bringing

you to the man and from that point on the work is done and the man takes over from there.

The man that God helps you to choose will know what to do to move the acquaintance from that point on because he now will be instructed by God about how to take the lead. So sisters, be encouraged and know that God will bring you to the man not the man to you. You can relax in the arms of God and know that " *all things work together for good to them that love God, to them who are the called according to his purpose.*" Romans 8:28

It's working for you right now if you will only believe it, receive it and conceive it in your spirit man then you shall have the manifestation of the man that God appoints in your life in the coming days.

2

God-Fearing verses Saved

"Let us hear the conclusion of the whole matter: Fear God, and keep his commandments: for this is the whole duty of man."

Today there are millions of individuals that name the name of Christ. If you were to ask most individuals they would tell you that they are saved and they believe in God. However, to just believe in God is not enough, the scripture says, **"The devil believes and trembles"** yet he is not God fearing to the point of obedience to his word. In St. John 3:16 a very familiar scripture says, *"For God so loved the world, that he gave his only begotten Son, that whosoever believeth in him should not perish, but have everlasting life."* The word believe here means to commit one's well being to Christ in obedience to his word, it doesn't mean just to have mental assent or agreement to the word but to yield your life in obedience to that word.

As a God-fearing Christian when you believe God for your Soul Mate you don't want someone that just say they believe in God or that they're saved. You want a God-fearing man that has a reverence for God and his word to the point of obedience in actually obeying and living the word. Here is the difference between a God-fearing man and a saved-man:

A SAVED MAN

- Saved---No real reverence for God/Carnal.
- God's Word – Only reads At Church.
- Church Attendance – Religious duty.
- Holy Living – Fornicates, Lies, Wickedness.
- Obedience – Walks in disobedience.

1. **Believes that they can't help but wilfully sin every now and then.**

2. **Believes that it's ok to miss church on a continuous basis.**

3. **Believes that bible reading is not that important.**

4. **Believes that prayer is only for the weak and ignorant.**

5. **Believes that church attendance is not**

that important and that's it's ok to miss bible study on a continuous basis.

6. Wants to see how much they can get away with and still believe they're saved.

7. Believes that it's okay to live a lifestyle of fornication.

8. Believes their righteousness is acceptable with God.

9. Have one foot in the world and one in the church.

10. Is far from the one great commandment of love. They don't love God and they will not know how to love you as Christ will have you to be loved.

A GOD FEARING MAN

- God-Fearing---A reverence for God
- God's Word — Studies and Reads
- Church Attendance — Faithful In Service
- Holy Living — Walks In Righteousness
- Obedience — Obeys the Word of God

1. **Believes that they have power over sin and that** *"sin shall not have dominion over them."* *Romans 6:14a*

2. **Believes that church attendance is of vital importance to their spiritual life and growth.**

3. **Believes that the bible is the word of God and that they must** *"Study to show thyself approved unto God, a workman that needeth not to be ashamed, rightly dividing the word of truth."*

4. **Believes that prayer is the key to relationship with God and** *"that man ought to always pray and not to faint."*

5. **Believes that we** *"should not forsake the assembling of ourselves together"* **but we**

should be glad to come into the house of the Lord.

6. Desires to walk in obedience to the word of God and mature and go on to know the Lord in a most intimate way.

7. Believes that their body is holy and *"the temple of the Holy Ghost which is in them, which they have of God, and they are not their own and that they "are bought with a price: therefore (they desires to) glorify God in their body, and in their spirit, which are God's." 1 Corinthians 6:19*

8. Believes that Christ is their righteousness and they have nothing to boast in themselves of *"for by grace are ye saved through faith; and that not of yourselves: it is the gift of God: Not of works, lest any man should boast." Ephesians 2:8-9*

9. Believes that they must *"put off concerning the former conversation of the*

old man, which is corrupt according to the deceitful lusts; And be renewed in the spirit of their mind. And that ye put on the new man, which after God is created in righteousness and true holiness." Ephesians 4:22-25

10. **Believes that love is the fulfilling of the law and that love is the greatest of all. They love God and walk in love and will therefore know how to love you. 1 Corinthians 13:**

Don't settle for someone that's just saved for that individual will bring you down and become one of the greatest liabilities to your spiritual life. A God-fearing person and a saved-person is not a match made in heaven but will put you at the very gates of hell and will be like mixing water and oil. The scripture tells us, *"Give not that which is holy unto the dogs, neither cast ye your pearls before swine, lest they trample them under their feet, and TURN AGAIN AND REND YOU." Matthew 7:6*

Why should a God-fearing woman give themselves over to one that can eventually become a thorn in their flesh? God has someone that is just right for you and will love you even as Christ loves the church. True, there are not a lot of God-fearing men but there is a God-fearing man that God has appointed for you. Refuse to settle for less than the best that God has for you. It is best to remain single than for a God-fearing woman to get tangled up with just a saved man. But thanks are to God because of the information in this book you will not have to remain single but you will find your Soul Mate and the love of your life.

3

Waiting on God, the Truth and Deception Behind It.

If you were to ask single Christian men and women about their singleness they will mostly respond by saying; *"I am waiting on God for my Soul Mate or marriage."* You will also discover that these same individuals have been single for 5, 10, and 20 years or more. Their explanation for their singleness is either that God is still working on them or God will send them their spouse in due time. What these individuals fail to realize is that first, God will always be working on them and there is a part of their character that will only be transformed through marriage.

Second, they fail to realize that they are not waiting on God but God is waiting on them. Unless these individuals get the proper knowledge and apply that knowledge they will be single for the next 5, 10, and 20 years or more. I know a young lady right now that desires to be married but have been waiting on God and her waiting period has already exceeded 25 years.

Individuals are thinking that the power of attracting their Soul Mate is totally in God's hand but this is a fallacy, this power is in the hands of both God and the individual. Yet, God will not allow or permit certain things to happen or manifest until we allow or permit certain things to happen or manifest. Also, God will not forbid or stop certain things from continuing until we forbid or stop certain things from continuing in our life. The scriptures say, *"Whatsoever thou shalt bind (or forbid) on earth shall be bound (or forbid) in heaven: and whatsoever thou shalt loose (or allow) on earth shall be loosed (allowed) in heaven."* Matthew 16:19b, 18:18

The allowing or forbidding of a thing starts on earth not in heaven. This is why an individual can continue in singleness for 10, 20 years or more, it's because they will not forbid or bind that spirit of continuation from continuing in their life, and therefore God will not forbid or bind it. But the moments that they will become partners with God and allow or loose the spirit of attraction to attract their Soul Mate God will begin to allow or loose that person to manifest in their life.

When this happen the person faith moves from a passive faith to an active faith and then they will have whatsoever they say. Mark 11:23 However, if they continue doing the same old thing they will continue to get the same results, you cannot expect different results following the same pattern. If you want something that you've never had then you must do something that you've never done.

Why should you be single when others are discovering the truths about how to find or be found of their Soul Mate? There is an individual at this very moment that is waiting on you. You are their Soul Mate, yet the two of you haven't met. The individual that you're longing for is also longing for you. However, one of you must get on the right track in understanding how to bring the two of you together. The key to everything is FAITH. And yes you do have a measure of faith and that measure is all you need to move every relationship mountain that you're now facing. Jesus said, *"If ye have faith as a grain of mustard seed, ye shall say unto this mountain, Remove hence to yonder place; and it shall remove; and nothing shall be impossible unto you."* Matthew 17:21

The missing ingredient is how you're using your faith. Most individuals have a passive faith. If you want to attract your Soul Mate you must leave the realm of passive faith and come into the realm of active faith. When you say such things as **"One day I will meet my Soul Mate, I believe I have a Soul Mate out there somewhere, He will find me in due time, I believe that I am going to meet the right man some day."** All of this is passive faith it is a futuristic belief that it will happen someday but not today. Active faith is totally different, this type put works behind its belief and this is the only kind that gets results.

Faith is now! Not in the future! Not one day or some day! In order for your faith to become an active faith you must now put yourself in the environment that you desire. Visualize you and your Soul Mate doing things that you will do when you're together. In other words get your mind and image off what you don't want and put it on what you do want. If you can capture this thought and idea I am giving you, within the idea itself is enough power to bring the idea into actual physical manifestation. It is not your obligation or duty to make it manifest or to figure out how it will come to pass. It is your obligation to simply have active faith that you have that which you believe. Keep your thoughts and focus upon the idea and visualization of you and your Soul Mate doing things together. Such things as going to the movies, going out to dinner, going to church, enjoying time alone, taking a nice walk in the park hand in hand, or just sitting on the couch together enjoying a movie. You must keep in mind that you're putting out your visualization to an omnipotent, to an omniscience and omnipresent God that knows exactly where your Soul Mate is. God is just waiting on you to have active faith so that he can produce for you in accordance with the kindred mate of your visualization. When your dominant thoughts are of what you want, and not what you don't want then God will reward your secret thoughts by reproducing them in physical form (your Soul Mate). God knows no such thing as failure and there is no such reality in the Spirit realm of asking and not receiving, of seeking and not finding, of knocking and no doors are opened. For all of creation is waiting for you to take your role as a Master of situations and no longer a slave of circumstances, for your inner thoughts and visualization will reflect your outer manifestation.

Here Are 7 Things You Must Do Immediately

1. Become Active In Your Faith
2. Seek first the kingdom of God and his righteousness.
3. Change your way of thinking from negative to positive about relationships, dating and your own situation.
4. Change the words you speak about relationships, dating and your own situation.
5. Begin to meditate about you and your Soul Mate.
6. Make yourself a Soul Mate Chart so that you can know what you want in a Soul Mate.
7. Praise God daily for your Soul Mate.

4

Divine Help In Finding Your Soul Mate

"Are they not all ministering spirits, sent forth to minister for them who shall be heirs of salvation."
Hebrews 1:14

In finding or being found of your Soul Mate you must realize that God has not left you alone in this endeavor. But he has sent you help and assistance by sending you the Comforter as Jesus stated, *"And I will pray the Father, and he shall give you another Comforter, that he may abide with you for ever; Even the Spirit of truth; whom the world cannot receive, because it seeth him not, neither knoweth him: but ye know him; for he dwelleth with you, and shall be in you. I will not leave you comfortless: I will come unto you. But the Comforter, which is the Holy Ghost, whom the Father will send in my name, he shall teach you all things, and bring all things to your remembrance, whatsoever I have said unto you."* John 14:16-18, 26

This is very good news that we're not alone and the Comforter walks and talks with us and teaches us in the way which we should go in life. The world may grope around in darkness going from one date to another, one marriage to another, not knowing how to find their Soul Mate but as Christians we don't have to settle for that. In the above Scripture there is something of vital interest that I think you missed, the word of God says, *"And I will pray the Father, and he shall give you another Comforter, that he may abide with you for ever; Even the Spirit of truth;* **whom the world cannot receive,** **(did you get that)** *because it seeth him not, neither knoweth him: but ye know him; for he dwelleth with you, and shall be in you."* John 11:17 The world are on their own, what a scary thought. But not you, you have divine help in finding your Soul Mate.

Yet, God did not stop there, he wants to make sure that you get it right this time or if this is your first marriage, the first time. In order to do that he has given you additional divine help to make sure that this time around you find your Soul Mate and not just another date. God in his wisdom has assigned to mankind angels that assist him in his great work. Angels are sent forth to minister on our behalf for we're heirs of salvation and they therefore assist us in our work. Angels are the divine helpers to assist you in life situations and circumstances.

- *Angels can go before you and prepare your way to make it prosperous. Exodus 23:20-22*
- *Angels can help you prosper in areas of your life. Psalms 91:11-12*
- *Angels can work on your behalf and help bring things to pass. Judges 6:11-22*
- *Angels are sent forth to minister on your behalf. Hebrews 1:14*

The word minister means to serve they will serve you in whatever capacity you need them to help you in, they will not do what you can do but they will help you in what you cannot do. We have failed to realize the assistance of angels; as a result we have omitted the help of God's secret agents. We do not have the authority or right to charge angels as some teach, this authority and right is assigned to God. Yet, we see angels in many capacities throughout the scriptures:

- *We see angels as they wait upon Christ. Luke 22:43*
- *We see angels as they help Abraham's servant find a wife for his son Isaac. Genesis 24:7, 40*

- *We see an angel speak to Jacob in a dream and give him a business idea of how to prosper. Genesis 31:9-13*
- *We see angels assigned to keep the saints from evil. Psalms 91:10-12*
- *We see how angels are assigned to God's people to bring them into the place God has prepared for them. Exodus 23:20*

Angels are the neglected agents of God that aren't doing a portion of the work they could be doing in the earth because man has failed to realize who they are, what they can do and how they can assist us in life. You can have divine help in finding your Soul Mate as you ask God to let his angels go forth and minister on your behalf to prosper you in your ways. We see this in the story when Abraham's servant went to find a wife for his son Isaac.

"AND ABRAHAM was old, and well stricken in age: and the LORD has blessed Abraham in all things. And Abraham said unto his eldest servant of his house, that ruled over all that he had, Put, I pray thee, thy hand under my thigh: And I will make thee swear by the LORD, the God of heaven, and the God of the earth, that thou shalt not take a wife unto my son of the daughters of the Canaanites, among whom I dwell: But thou shalt go unto my country, and to my kindred, and

take a wife unto my son Isaac. And the servant said unto him, Peradventure the woman will not be willing to follow me unto this land: must I needs bring thy son again unto the land from whence thou camest? And Abraham said unto him, Beware thou that thou bring not my son thither again. The LORD God of heaven, which took me from my father's house, and from the land of my kindred, and which spake unto me, and that sware unto me, saying, Unto thy seed will I give this land; **he shall send his angel before thee,** and thou shalt take a wife unto my son from thence." Genesis 24:1-7 Well we know the conclusion of the story, Isaac received his wife Rebekah and she was his Soul Mate. Angels will do the same for you when you understand how God has assigned them to work on your behalf.

The angels of God can assist you in many situations and circumstances that may be held back from you by the hand of the enemy. The scripture says, "For we wrestle not against flesh and blood, but against principalities, against powers, against the rulers of the darkness of this world, against spiritual wickedness in high places." Ephesians 6:12 Let me inform you of something that you may not be aware of:

- *If you are 50 and over and you have never*

been married but desire to be married you are probably under a demonic attack that is hindering you from finding your Soul Mate.

- *If you have been married 3, 4, 5, times and can't seem to get it right and keep attracting the wrong kind of men you are probably also under a demonic attack that is keeping the right man from you.*

- *If your relationships all keep going bad and you're meeting good people then you're probably under a demonic attack that is stopping your progress in the relationship area of your life.*

- *If you just can't seem to attract the right man to save your life and you've been single for many years, you're probably under a demonic attack that is hindering you from going forward in the relationship area of your life.*

Yes the devil and demons are real and they care nothing for you and will do anything to stop your progress in relationships and in life. They want to steal away from you anyone that will be good for you. They want to kill off all the good relationships and individuals that will be an asset to your life.

- Finally, they want to destroy your self-esteem by making you feel belittled and believe that you'll never find the right person and you will be single all your life. **THE DEVI IS A LIAR!** The Scripture says, *"The thief (that old devil) cometh not, but for to steal, and to kill, and to destroy. I am come that they might have life, and that they might have it more abundantly"* John 10:10 God wants to send the angel to assist you in finding your Soul Mate.

Your Soul Mate may have been held up from you, your prayers may have been hindered because satanic forces have blocked your good from coming and you have not asked God to let his angel's minister on your behalf to help you. In the book of Daniel we see how the answer to his prayers were held up by satanic forces that blocked the way from him receiving his answers, but the angels of God assisted Daniel and brought the answer forth.

"Then said he unto me, Fear not, Daniel: for from the first day that thou didst set thine heart to understand, and to chasten thyself before thy God, thy words were heard, and I am come for thy words. But the prince of

the kingdom of Persia withstood me one and twenty days: but, lo, Michael, one of the chief princes, came to help me; and I remained there with the kings of Persia. Now I am come to make thee understand what shall befall thy people in the latter days: for yet the vision is for many days. Then said he, Knowest thou wherefore I am come unto thee? and now I will return to fight with the prince of Persia: and when I am gone forth, lo, the prince of Grecia shall come." Daniel 10:12-14, 20-21

It's time to put the devil to a flight in your life and especially your relationship life. You shouldn't be 50 years old and have never been married or over 50 and think your relationship life is over. THE DEVIL IS A LIAR! Angels can give you divine help in your relationship life where assistance is definitely needed and here is a prayer that I like to pray in asking God for divine help in the assistance of angels. You can make it your own.

AFFIRMATION OR PRAYER

"Heavenly Father, I give you praise and thanks for your goodness and mercy. I thank you for being the LORD that exerciseth lovingkindness judgment and righteousness in the earth. Jeremiah 9:24 I acknowledge you today and I need your help in all things. You said in all our ways to acknowledge you and you will direct our

paths. Proverbs 3:6 Father, I ask you today to send forth your angels to minister on my behalf for I am an heir of salvation. I am not sufficient of myself as to think anything of myself, but my sufficiency is of thee. 2 Corinthians 3:5

Father, according to your word you have given your angels charge over me to keep me in all my ways, today I need you to let your angels minister on my behalf to help me find my Soul Mate and life mate. Even as you did with Abraham servant in helping him find a wife for his son Isaac. In your word you said Know ye therefore that they which are of faith, the same are the children of Abraham. Saying, In thee shall all nations be blessed. So then they which be of faith are blessed with faithful Abraham. That the blessing of Abraham might come on the Gentiles through Jesus Christ. And if ye be Christ's, then are ye Abraham's seed, and heirs according to the promise." Galatians 3:7-8b, 9, 14a, 29

Thank you heavenly Father for your blessings now, I believe it and receive it now and I shall have what I desire. Thank you for your faithfulness, for your word will not go out and return void but it shall accomplish that which it was sent to do and it shall prosper therein, in Jesus name Amen. Isaiah

Now begin to visualize and see yourself in the

act of receiving that which you have requested of God by faith, see the angels going forth and ministering on your behalf for you're an heir of salvation. See the angels in your imagination going forth and doing exactly that which you've asked God to send them forth to do. See yourself already with your Soul Mate. See your Soul Mate and you doing things together just as if your request was answered in reality and then you shall have that which you requested.

5

The Spirit Man

"The spirit of man is the candle of the LORD, searching all the inward parts of the belly." Proverbs 20:27

The spirit of man is the real man. If you can get the revelation of this book in your spirit man, next time this year you will either be walking down the aisle or getting ready to walk down the aisle to say I DO!

This is a true statement not just some pie in the sky theory or some hypothesis, it is the truth, the whole truth and nothing but the truth so help me God. We presented a question to several singles during a discussion that we had and asked them about their desire to be married and how they see their future. Out of the ten singles there was only one that had the note of victory in their answer. When we left the restaurant on that evening I mentioned to my wife that there was only one person at the table that would be getting married soon, well less than one month from the date of this book coming out that individual is getting ready to walk down the aisle to say I DO! The rest of the singles about a year later are still single with no real prospects in sight. What was the difference between the answer of that individual and the answer from the rest of the individuals that were so different? That one individual had conceived the idea of marriage in their spirit while the other individuals had only mental assent to the word of God and their belief. The others individuals were confessing with their mouth, but (the belief) in their heart (spirit) were far from the confession of their mouth and the mental assent in their mind.

You have to see yourself married before you see it or you will never see it in the external world of reality. You have to see it through the eyes of faith and the reality of it must be real in your spirit and not just a confession of your mouth and an agreement of your mind.

Nothing is real except that which is a reality in your spirit, whether good or bad, positive or negative, truth or a lie. When it gets in your spirit then and only then will it manifest in your life. Nothing else is going to get you where you need to be except you learn the truth that you must begin to do things from the spirit man and not just from your mind. How can one person find their soul mate in so brief a period of time while others have desired to be married for years but haven't gotten married yet? It doesn't take God 10, 20 and 30 years to find you a mate. It only took him 6 days to create the world and man but you're such a unique case that it's taking him 10, 20 years or more. The devil is a liar!

The word of God says, *"But there is a spirit in man: and the inspiration of the Almighty giveth them understanding." Proverbs 32:8* When you get inspired in your spirit by the Almighty God then as sure as the night follows the day you shall have what you desire. The word of God also says, *"For verily I say unto you, That whosoever shall say unto this mountain,* **(this mountain of singleness when you desire to be married***) Be thou removed, and be thou cast into the sea; and shall not doubt in his heart, but shall believe that those things which he saith shall come to pass; he shall have whatsoever he saith. Therefore I say unto you, What things soever ye desire, when ye pray, believe that ye receive them, and ye shall have them." Mark 11:23-24* The word heart in this passage of scripture is translated spirit and when you believe and receive and that belief is conceived in your spirit then you are operating with the faith of God and every mountain has to move. When you get the belief that you shall be married in your spirit and you can say with 100% confidence that I shall be married then marriage for you is right around the corner. Most individual think they have this 100% confidence in God to manifest their desires but their spirit man is saying something different than their head and their mouth **(for a greater revelation See our book, "Soul Mate or Just Another Date.)** But when you can say within yourself that I know that I know that I know I shall be married next year this time, then sister you might as well start looking for your dress and planning your bridal party because you shall be married.

You have probably heard of the story of the lady with the issue of blood; however there is a revelation in this passage that you may have missed that pertains to the spirit man. So the story goes, *"And, behold, a woman, which was diseased with an issue of blood twelve years, And had suffered many things of many physicians, and had spent all that she had, and was nothing bettered, but rather grew worse, came behind him, and touched the hem of his garment: For she said within herself, If I may but touch his garment, I shall be whole. And straightway the fountain of her blood was dried up; and she felt in her body that she was healed of that plague. And Jesus said, Who touched me? When all denied, Peter and they that were with him said, Master, the multitude throng thee and press thee, and sayest thou, Who touched me? And Jesus said, Somebody hath touched me: for I perceive that virtue is gone out of me. And when the woman saw that she was not hid, she came trembling, and falling down before him, she declared unto him before all the people for what cause she had touched him, and how she was healed immediately. And he said unto her, Daughter, be of good comfort: thy faith hath made thee whole; go in peace."* Matthew 9:20, Mark 5:26, Luke 8:45-48

It said that the woman **said within herself**, in other words she spoke out of her spirit and said, *"If I may but touch his garment, I shall be whole."* Listen at this woman speaking forth boldly with confidence. The majority of the time when individuals speak about marriage they have a take it or leave it attitude and speech. Their mind is unstable in their decision, one day they want to get married and the next day they don't want to get married. The Bible speaks about such a person saying," *But let him ask in faith, nothing wavering. For he that wavereth is like a wave of the sea driven with the wind and tossed. For let not that man think that he shall receive any thing of the Lord. A double minded man* *is unstable in all his ways."* James 1:6-8 Do you want to get married or don't you? You can't be marriage minded one day and single minded the next day. This woman was not doubled minded in her decision to be healed she had a single mind with one focus, **I shall be made whole**. Likewise if marriage is what you desire and if you're reading this book then it must be, you likewise must have a single mind with one focus, **I shall be married.**

When you get that mind in your spirit then you will touch God with your belief, and inspiration and power will come from the Almighty and he will bring you to that man that he has appointed for you and say to you, *Daughter, be of good comfort: thy faith hath produced for you your husband; go in peace.*

One of the methods of getting this belief conceived in your spirit man is understanding the concept of what happens at night when you sleep. The scripture says, *"I call to remembrance my song in the night: I commune with mine own heart: and my spirit made diligent search." Psalms 77:6*

Because man is a tri-fold being and consists of spirit, soul and body, each part of man has its particular function and operation, but when all parts are working harmoniously and in totality then mankind is at their best. Yet, in the midst of their makeup we discover that two out of the three of their tri-fold being must eventually come to a halt and shut down in order to rest.

The soul of man which a part houses his mind from which derives his thoughts, emotions and intellect works in connection with his brain which is the master control nucleus of the body. The brain receives information from the senses both about the inside and outside of the body. It takes this information and quickly analyzes it, and then sends out messages that control the body actions and functions. The brain is also the information center that stores past experiences which makes learning and remembering possible.

The human brain consist of billions of interconnected cells which enables people to be creative, use language, plan and solve difficult problems. A network of blood vessels supplies the brain with the vast quantities of oxygen and food that it requires. The brain of man is a most powerful thing yet it's not omnipotent and the brain must have a time of rest and sleep. When a person deprives themselves of sleep for an extended period of time, the brain becomes fuzzy and the person thinking began to deteriorate and becomes distorted. A person therefore must get a certain amount of sleep in order for the brain to function at its optimum so that it can be creative, make learning and remembering flow fluently and planning and solving problems possible. Sleep also stills the conscious part of man and quite his consciousness so that his spirit can work without the interference of his conscious mind.

The body of man, which consists of his outward physical makeup, must also have a certain amount of rest and sleep without it the body becomes deprived of its vitality and health. When the body does not get its proper rest and sleep it begins to feel sluggish and lethargy the once energetic person now feels drains and exhausted. The body is trying to tell you that it must get rest and sleep in order to be revived and energized, if the body continue on its deprived and needy course permanent damage can occur and serious consequences of health problems will be the result.

The spirit of man is that part of man that neither slumbers nor sleeps and the omnipotent and omniscience presence of God dwells within your spirit. Your spirit never sleeps day or night the spirit can go nonstop without rest or sleep, Jesus said it best saying *"the spirit indeed is willing, but the flesh is weak, the spirit truly is ready, but the flesh is weak." Matthew 26:41, Mark 14:38b*

Because your spirit never slumbers nor sleep you have been endowed with an awesome power that can help chart your destiny in every phase of your life. You can influence your spirit for good, success, marriage, increase, prosperity and wealth by speaking to your spirit man at the time when he is most accessible and open to influence. Your spirit which never sleeps is more open to your prayers, suggestions, commands and affirmations just prior to sleep than any other time because your conscious mind has become quite and silent. During sleep your spirit, which never sleeps, is not challenged by your conscious mind.

During sleep your spirit can more easily get you answers to prayers and even suggestions and commands that you make just prior to your dosing off. During sleep your spirit can also bring you solutions to problems that may have been hard to come by. I am reminded of how one of my books in particular came into existence *the book Hidden Riches of Secret Places was given to me in a dream, in this dream I was riding on a bus and on the bus was another young man that I know and respect as a man of God, as I was sitting behind him he turned around and looked at me and made this one simple statement that changed the course of my life and thinking about finances. The statement was,* **"The human body and finances work the same. If you can understand the working of the human body finances work the same way."** *(See our book:* **Hidden Riches of Secret Places***)*

This was obviously a message that God wanted my spirit to receive but my conscious mind may have blocked it out from coming up so that I couldn't perceive it. Yet on that particular night of sleep my conscious mind was still and God revealed it to my spirit which never sleeps and it came forth in a dream. On many occasions, I have gotten answers that I needed in a dream or either during times of meditation when my conscious mind was still and God was able to speak in my spirit and bring it forth in a dream or in a still small voice in my spirit where I was able to perceive it clearly. 1 Kings

19:11-13 On many occasions throughout Scripture, we see God speaking to men in dreams and visions revealing to them answers in many areas present and future. Seeing that God dwells in our spirit this is where he communicate to us on some occasions his plans, answers and purposes. He reveals many things in dreams and visions of the night.

He revealed in a dream the vision of Jacob's ladder, so it goes *"And he (Jacob) dreamed, and behold a ladder set up on the earth, and the top of it reached to heaven: and behold the angels of God ascending and descending on it. And, behold, the LORD stood above it, and said, I am the LORD God of Abraham thy father, and the God of Isaac: the land whereon thou liest, to thee will I give it, and to thy seed; And thy seed shall be as the dust of the earth; and thou shalt spread abroad to the west, and to the east, and to the north, and to the south: and in thee and in thy seed shall all the families of the earth be blessed. And, behold, I am with thee, and will keep thee in all places whither thou goest, and will bring thee again into this land; for I will not leave thee, until I have done that which I have spoken to thee of. And Jacob awaked out of his sleep, and he said, Surely the LORD is in this place; and I knew it not." Genesis 28:12-16* Also, we see in the book of Daniel how he needed immediate answers to the king's dream, *"Then Daniel went in, and desired of the king that he would give him time, and that he would shew the king the interpretation. Then Daniel went to his house, and made the thing known to Hananiah, Mishael, and Azariah, his companions: That they would desire mercies of the God of heaven* **concerning this secret***; that Daniel and his fellows should not perish with the rest of the wise men of Babylon. Then was the secret revealed unto Daniel in a night vision. Then Daniel blessed the God of heaven (saying).* **He revealeth the deep and secret things: he knoweth what is in the darkness, and the light dwelleth with him.***" Daniel 2:16-23*

Here we see Daniel and his companions asking the God of heaven to reveal this secret, we do not know whether Daniel and his companions prayed right before they went to sleep but we do know that it was revealed in a night vision. Throughout the scriptures we see many things revealed in dreams and visions, many times this is God's great time to speak to man and confirm or answer man's request, prayers or affirmations. One of the reasons is because at this time man's consciousness is less active and his spirit is more open and receptive to divine intervention, spiritual things and your own spirit's voice. Within your spirit lies awesome ability to perform many things because of the simple fact that your spirit as a born again Christian is alive towards God and more tuned to the voice of God and the Spirit of God have freer access to lead and guide you. As a Christian, you have a divine connection and your spirit is the gauge that connects you to God.

- *"The spirit of man is the candle of the LORD, searching all the inward parts of the belly."* Proverbs 20:27

- *"The Spirit itself beareth witness with our spirit, that we are the children of God."* Romans 8:16

- *"That which is born of the flesh is flesh; and that which is born of the Spirit is spirit."* John 3:6

- *"But ye are not in the flesh, but in the Spirit, if so be that the Spirit of God dwell in you. Now if any man have not the Spirit of Christ, he is none of his."* Romans 8:9

God can speak to your spirit in many ways for your spirit is strong because God dwells there.

1. *Within your spirit is the ability to make a million dollars. 1 Corinthians 2:9 10*

2. *Within your spirit is the ability to know the future. St. John 16:13*

3. *Within your spirit is the ability to overcome every sin. Romans 6:14*

4. *Within your spirit is the ability to heal your body. Proverbs 18:14*

5. *Within your spirit is the ability to worship God. St. John 4:24*

6. *Within your spirit is the ability to pray in an unknown tongue. 1 Corinthians 14:14*

7. *Within your spirit is the ability to sing with the spirit. 1 Corinthians 14:15*

8. *Within your spirit is omniscience wisdom and your spirit knows all things already. For "ye have an unction from the Holy One, and ye know all things." 1 John 2:20*

From this day forward begin the process of stiring up your spirit to make it strong and more receptive to the things and leading of God. You do this by meditating in the word of God. *"When I remember thee upon my bed, and meditate on thee in the night watches."* Psalm 63:6, Psalms 1:2, 77:2, 119:15, 119:23, 119:48, 119:78, 119:148, Joshua 1:8, 1 Timothy 4:15

You do this by prayer and praying in the Holy Ghost. *"But ye, beloved, building up yourselves on your most holy faith, praying in the Holy Ghost."* Jude 1:20

You do this by reading and studying the word of God. *"Study to shew thyself approved unto God a workman that needeth not to be ashamed, rightly dividing the word of truth."* 2 Timothy 2:15, Hebrews 4:12, Ephesians 1:17-18 Your spirit man also become strong as you attend the place of worship and hear the word of God, as you listen to the word preached or taught by various means of audio, video, CD etc. Ephesians 4:8-16

Also, you build up your spirit by having a daily confession of the word of God in your mouth using affirmations to build up your inward man. *"For which cause we faint not; but though our outward man perish, yet the inward man is renewed day by day."* 2 Corinthians 4:16, Romans 7:22, 2 Corinthians 4:16, James 3:2, Proverbs 6:2, Genesis 1:3-24, Proverbs 18:21

Never fail to realize the power of your sleepless spirit always ready to avail you of answers, solutions and directions for your life. Within your spirit abides the awesome Spirit of God and you know all things, begin to allow God to speak to your spirit and direct your steps for *"ye have an unction from the Holy One, and ye know all things. But the anointing which ye have received of him abideth in you, and ye need not that any man teach you: but the same anointing teacheth you of all things, and is truth, and is no lie, and even as it hath taught you, ye shall abide in him."* 1 John 2:20, 27

6

On Again / Off Again Relationships

"My son, fear thou the LORD and the king: and meddle not with them that are given to change." Proverbs 24:21

If you're in a relationship and you're wondering whether it's of God or not, one thing you want to understand is that if there are too many negatives in the relationship and it has constantly been an on again off again relationship, you already have your answer. Just receive it. If you still can't receive it well here are some cold hard truths?

On again / off again relationships are designed to turn your emotional world upside down. We all at one time or another have been in a relationship where the connection has been on at time and off at times. The off times of the relationship were times that brought about a rift in the connection. No relationships are going to be without its challenges and disagreements. It's ok to disagree but mature individuals learn how to disagree without being disagreeable. Immature individuals disagree and either calls it quits or part ways with much animosity and hostility. The truth about on again/off again relationships are that they create much frustration and a whirlwind of emotional chaos and confusion. On again/off again relationships are designed to turn your emotional world upside down and keep you in a state of disillusionment and opposition that can even turn into hatred.

On again / off again relationships rarely end up a happy relationship and the two parties end up with a broken heart and broken promises. Now let's look at some hard cold truths:

- *Somebody in the relationship doesn't want to really be with the other.*

- *The reason that your relationship is on again/off again is because the interest level that you have in each other is not high enough to create a true bond. One of your interest levels is high and the other is low.*

- *Things are good for a while a month or so and then you are right back where you started.*

- *You think you have a bond because of the longevity of your relationship but it's a farce, a foolish show, a mockery and a ridiculous sham. (I wish I could tell you this is going to get more to your liking but it's not.)*

- *The reason you continue in this foolishness is because you are opposites and you believe the lie that opposites attract and are good for each other. All opposites do is attract each other but they have no power to make good on it or produce substance out of the relationship.*

- *The two of you are simply pretending to have a good relationship but deep down you know you want out because it's empty, dead, void and keep you on an emotional roller coaster ride.*

- *This on again/off again relationship is nothing but a yo-yo connection and it has already created years of torture for you.*

- *It's not a match made in heaven but a match made in hell and if it doesn't literally send you to hell it will keep you living in hell on earth.*

- *Somebody is simply stringing the other along, besides they know you will be back because you have already been back 20 plus times what does one more time matter. Then this one more time turns into one more time, then one more time turns into one more time, then one more time turns into one more time, then one more time turns into one more time etc... How many times are you going to split up before you wake up and smell the coffee as they say? Let go and get on with your life. God did not create you for this mess.*

The scripture says, *"The thief (the devil) cometh but to steal, and to kill, and to destroy: I am come (Jesus) that they (you) might have life, and that they (you) might have it more abundantly."* John 10:10 The devil is using your on again / off again relationship to steal the joy out of your life, to kill off your emotional well-being and to eventually destroy your life and your pursuit of happiness. Jesus has come to give you joy, the life of God and to give it to you in such an abundance that you can spend your days living life to the fullest in every aspect of your life. There is a great relationship and a great person out there for you, but you must decide if you will continue with your on again/off again relationship for another year or will you make this your year of change. If you don't have enough fortitude or mental and emotional will power and strength to do it for yourself then do it for your children (if children are involved in your life) or your family who is tired of seeing your life in turmoil and difficulty.

7

Twelve Authoritative Prayers To Bind And Blast Away Just Another Date

"And whatsoever you shall bind on earth shall be bound in heaven." Matthew 16:19

Here are 12 Authoritative prayers that you can use to bind and blast away just more dates. From this day forward begin to take authority over your relationship life and determine your destiny by orchestrating it in prayer. At this point go to God in prayer and confess any known sin to the Lord and repent of anything that may stand between you and God. Ask him to forgive you and cleanse you by his precious blood.

Next, take about 5 minutes and begin to spend time in praises to the Lord, thanking him for who he is and what he has done for you and what he shall do for you in orchestrating the destiny of you and your soul mate. Now, enter into this time of prayer with aggressive and bold praying. Pray the prayers repeatedly with determination and faith until you see the manifestation of your desire.

The Prayer

1. I bind just more dates from coming into my life from this day forward in Jesus name.

2. I refuse to waste my time with individuals that aren't sent by God to be in my life in the name of Jesus.

3. No weapon that is formed against me shall prosper in the name of Jesus.

4. I reject unrighteous associations that try to become a part of my life in Jesus name.

5. I release myself from the spirit of divorces and unstable relationships in the name of Jesus.

6. Every spirit of instability in relationships I detach myself from you in the name of Jesus.

7. I break the spirit of familiarity that has caused me to attach myself to people that have been wrong for me in the past in the name of Jesus.

8. Every satanic influence that has led me astray in relationships the hand of God is against you in Jesus name.

9. Every satanic deception; the fire of God is against you in Jesus name.

10. Every seducing spirit; the Lord rebukes you in Jesus name.

11. Every hidden agenda come to light and is bound in Jesus name.

12. I reject all that are transformed as an angle of light, but are sent by Satan to destroy and prevent my true marital destiny in Jesus name.

8

Twelve Authoritative Prayers to Loose And Attract Your Soul Mate

"And whatsoever ye shall loose on earth shall be loosed in heaven." Matthew 16:19

Here are 12 Authoritative Prayers you can use to Loose and Attract Your Soul Mate. Pray these prayers in the same manner which you prayed the prayers above and watch God attract to you your soul mate and life mate.

1. **I loose the Spirit of God to attract to me the individual that God has destined to be my soul mate and life mate in the name of Jesus.**

2. **Father, I commit my life to you and thank you for directing me toward the individual that is my soul mate in Jesus name.**

3. **Father, I give you praise that I'm hidden under your shadow so that only my soul**

mate can find me in Jesus name.

4. The blood of Jesus protects me from every encounter that's not the destiny of my soul mate and I in the name of Jesus.

5. My relationship life lives now by the resurrection power of the Lord Jesus Christ.

6. The Holy Spirit of God leads me into all truth in relationships in Jesus name.

7. The angel of the Lord encamps about me and delivers me from every satanic plan in the name of Jesus.

8. Father, I thank you for stretching forth your mighty hand to perform signs and wonders in my relationship life in Jesus name.

9. My prayer now attracts to me the soul mate that God has destined to be in my life in the name of Jesus.

10. The anointing of God destroys every yoke that comes against me in Jesus name.

11. Father, I thank you for your divine intervention on my behalf in the name of Jesus.

12. Lord, thank you for releasing the spirit of attraction that attracts to me my ideal soul mate in the name of Jesus.

9

The Song of Solomon

"The voice of my beloved! Behold, he cometh leaping upon the mountains, skipping upon the hills. My beloved is like a roe or a young hart: behold, he standeth behind our wall, he looketh forth at the windows, shewing himself through the lattice. My beloved spake, and said unto me, Rise up, my love, my fair one, and come away." Song of Solomon 2:8-10

The closest idea we have of a harmonious and compatible relationship of two people in love is exemplified in the scriptures according to the Song of Solomon. Here we have two people that are obviously soul mates. The communication and attraction between these two people displays love of the highest order; it shows respect, consideration, passion, compassion, kindness, unselfishness, patience, temperance, faith, hope and belief. Notice the terminology which they use and the easy display of verbal affection to one another, the honesty, sincerity and excitement of just being in one another's presence. We don't attempt to interpret the words of these two individuals that are wonderfully in love. Our objective is to just give it to you as it is and allow the Holy Spirit to enlighten your mind and speak to your spirit as you read it. Notice the love and beauty of it all as we listen to two people that are immensely in love with one another as it should be. Listen as the emotions run high and the feelings of each are spoken effortlessly. There is no holding back here because each desires the other to know what they think and how they feel. Read it slowly and observe the words they're speaking.

Let us now behold "The song of songs, which is Solomon's. Let him kiss me with the kisses of his mouth: for thy love is better than wine. Because of the savour of thy good ointments thy name is as ointment poured forth, therefore do the virgins love thee. Draw me, we will run after thee: the king hath brought me into his chambers: we will be glad and rejoice in thee, we will remember thy love more than wine: the upright love thee. I am black, but comely, O ye daughters of Jerusalem, as the tents of Kedar, as the curtains of Solomon. Look not upon me, because I am black, because the sun hath looked upon me: my mother's children were angry with me; they made me the keeper of the vineyards; but mine own vineyard have I not kept.

Tell me, O thou whom my soul loveth, where thou

feedest, where thou makest thy flock to rest at noon: for why should I be as one that turneth aside by the flocks of thy companions? If thou know not, O thou fairest among women, go thy way forth by the footsteps of the flock, and feed thy kids beside the shepherds' tents. I have compared thee, O my love, to a company of horses in Pharaoh's chariots. Thy cheeks are comely with rows of jewels, thy neck with chains of gold. We will make thee borders of gold with studs of silver. While the king sitteth at his table, my spikenard sendeth forth the smell thereof. A bundle of myrrh is my well-beloved unto me; he shall lie all night betwixt my breasts. My beloved is unto me as a cluster of camphire in the vineyards of En-gedi. Behold, thou art fair, my love; behold, thou art fair; thou hast doves' eyes. Behold, thou art fair, my beloved, yea, pleasant: also our bed is green. The beams of our house are cedar, and our rafters of fir. I am the rose of Sharon, and the lily of the valleys. As the lily among thorns, so is my love among the daughters. As the apple tree among the trees of the wood, so is my beloved among the sons. I sat down under his shadow with great delight, and his fruit was sweet to my taste. He brought me to the banqueting house, and his banner over me was love. Stay me with flagons, comfort me with apples: for I am sick of love. His left hand is under my head, and his right hand doth embrace me. I charge you, O ye daughters of Jerusalem, by the roes, and by the hinds of the field, that ye stir not up, nor awake my love, till he please.

The voice of my beloved! behold, he cometh leaping upon the mountains, skipping upon the hills. My beloved is like a roe or a young hart: behold, he standeth behind our wall, he looketh forth at the windows, shewing himself through the lattice. My beloved spake, and said unto me, Rise up, my love, my fair one, and come away. For, lo, the winter is past, the rain is over and gone; The flowers appear on the earth; the time of the singing of birds is come, and the voice of the turtle is heard in our land; The fig tree putteth forth her green figs, and the vines with the tender grape give a good smell. Arise, my love, my fair one, and come away. O my dove, that art in the clefts of the rock, in the secret places of the stairs, let me see thy countenance, let me hear thy voice; for sweet is thy voice, and thy countenance is comely.

Take us the foxes, the little foxes, that spoil the vines: for our vines have tender grapes. My beloved is mine, and I am his: he feedeth among the lilies. Until the day break, and the shadows flee away, turn, my beloved, and be thou like a roe or a young hart upon the mountains of Bether. By night on my bed I sought him whom my soul loveth: I sought him, but I found him not. I will rise now, and go *about the city in the streets, and in the broad ways I will seek him whom my soul loveth: I sought him, but I found him not. The watchmen that go about the city found me: to whom I said, Saw ye him whom my soul loveth? It was but a little that I passed from them, but I found him whom my soul loveth: I held him, and would not let him go, until I had brought him into my mother's house, and into the chamber of her that conceived me. I charge you, O ye daughters of Jerusalem, by the roes, and by the hinds of the field, that ye stir not up, nor awake my love, till he please.*

Who is this that cometh out of the wilderness like pillars of smoke, perfumed with myrrh and frankincense, with all powders of the merchant? Behold his bed, which is Solomon's; threescore valiant men are about it, of the valiant of Israel. They all hold swords, being expert in war: every man hath his sword upon his thigh because of fear in the night. King Solomon made himself a chariot of the wood of Lebanon. He made pillars thereof of silver, the bottom thereof of gold, the covering of it of purple, the midst thereof being paved with love, for the daughters of Jerusalem. Go forth, O ye daughters of Zion, and behold king Solomon with the crown wherewith his mother crowned him in the day of his espousals, and in the day of the gladness of his heart.

Behold, thou art fair, my love; behold, thou art fair; thou hast doves' eyes within thy locks: thy hair is as a flock of goats, that appear from mount Gilead. Thy teeth are like a flock of sheep that are even shorn, which came up from the washing; whereof every one bear twins, and none is barren among them. Thy lips are like a thread of scarlet, and thy speech is comely: thy temples are like a piece of a pomegranate within thy locks. Thy neck is like the tower of David builded for an armoury, whereon there hang a thousand bucklers, all shields of mighty men. Thy two breasts are like two young roes that are twins, which feed among the lilies. Until the day break, and the shadows flee away, I will get me to the mountain of myrrh, and to the hill of frankincense. Thou art all fair, my love; there is no spot in thee. Come with me from Lebanon, my spouse, with me from Lebanon: look from the top of Amana, from the top of Shenir and Hermon, from the lions' dens, from the mountains of the leopards. Thou hast ravished my heart, my sister, my spouse; thou hast ravished my heart with one of thine eyes, with one chain of thy neck. How fair is thy love, my sister, my spouse! How much better is thy love than wine! and the smell of thine ointments than all spices! Thy lips, O my spouse, drop as the honeycomb: honey and milk are under thy tongue; and the smell of thy garments is like the smell of Lebanon. A garden inclosed is my sister, my spouse; a spring shut up, a fountain sealed. Thy plants are an orchard of pomegranates, with pleasant fruits; camphire, with spikenard, Spikenard and saffron; calamus and cinnamon, with all trees of frankincense; myrrh and aloes, with all the chief spices: A fountain of gardens, a well of living waters, and streams from Lebanon. Awake, O north wind; and come, thou south; blow upon my garden, that the spices thereof may flow out. Let my beloved come into his garden and eat his pleasant fruits.

I am come into my garden, my sister, my spouse: I have gathered my myrrh with my spice; I have eaten my honeycomb with my honey; I have drunk my wine with my milk: eat, O friends; drink, yea, drink abundantly, O beloved. I sleep, but my heart waketh: it is the voice of my beloved that knocketh, saying, Open to me, my sister, my love, my dove, my undefiled: for my head is filled with dew, and my locks with the drops of the night. I have put off my coat; how shall I put it on? I have washed my feet; how shall I defile them? My beloved put in his hand by the hole of the door, and my bowels were moved for him. I rose up to open to my beloved; and my hand dropped with myrrh, and my fingers with sweet smelling myrrh, upon the handles of the lock I opened to my beloved; but my beloved had withdrawn himself, and was gone: my soul failed when he spake: I sought him, but I could not find him; I called him, but he gave me no answer. The *watchmen that went about the city found me, they smote me, they wounded me; the keepers of the walls took away my veil from me. I charge you, O daughter of Jerusalem, if ye find my beloved, that ye tell him, that I am sick of love.*

What is thy beloved more than another beloved, O thou fairest among women? what is thy beloved more than another beloved, that thou dost so charge us? My beloved is white and ruddy, the chiefest among ten thousand. His head is as the most fine gold, his locks are bushy, and black as a raven. His eyes are as the eyes of doves by the rivers of water, washed with milk, and fitly set. His cheeks are as a bed of spices, as sweet flowers: his lips like lilies, dropping sweet smelling myrrh. His hands are as gold rings set with the beryl: his belly is as bright ivory overlaid with sapphires. His legs are as pillars of marble, set upon sockets of fine gold: his countenance is as Lebanon, excellent as the cedars.

His mouth is most sweet: yea, he is altogether lovely. This is my beloved, and this is my friend, O daughters of Jerusalem. Whither is thy beloved gone, O thou fairest among women? whither is thy beloved turned aside? that we may seek him with thee. My beloved is gone down into his garden, to the bed of spices, to feed in the gardens, and to gather lilies. I am my beloved's, and my beloved is mine: he feedeth among the lilies. Thou art beautiful,

O my love, as Tirzah, comely as Jerusalem, terrible as an army with banners. Turn away thine eyes from me, for they have overcome me: thy hair is as a flock of goats that appear from Gilead. Thy teeth are as a flock of sheep which go up from the washing, whereof every one beareth twins, and there is not one barren among them. As a piece of a pomegranate are thy temples within thy locks. There are threescore queens, and fourscore concubines, and virgins without number. My dove, my undefiled is but one; she is the only one of her mother, she is the choice one of her that bare her. The daughters saw her, and blessed her; yea, the queens and the concubines, and they praised her. Who is she that looketh forth as the morning, fair as the moon, clear as the sun, and terrible as an army with banners? I went down into the garden of nuts to see the fruits of the valley, and to see whether the vine flourished, and the pomegranates budded. Or ever I was aware, my soul made me like the chariots of Ammi-nadib. Return, return, O Shulamite; return, return, that we may look upon thee. What will ye see in the Shulamite? As it were the company of two armies. How beautiful are thy feet with shoes, O prince's daughter! the joints of thy thighs are like jewels, the work of the hands of a cunning workman. Thy navel is like a round goblet, which wanteth not liquor: thy belly is like an heap of wheat set about with lilies. Thy two breasts are like two young roes that are twins. *Thy neck is as a tower of ivory: thine eyes like the fishpools in Heshbon, by the gate of Bath-rabbim: thy nose is as the tower of Lebanon which looketh toward Damascus. Thine head upon thee is like Carmel, and the hair of thine head like purple; the king is held in the galleries. How fair and how pleasant art thou, O love, for delights! This thy stature is like to a palm tree, and thy breasts to clusters of grapes. I said, I will go up to the palm tree, I will take hold of the boughs thereof: now also thy breasts shall be as the clusters of the vine, and the smell of thy nose like apples; And the roof of thy mouth like the best wine for my beloved, that goeth down sweetly, causing the lips of those that are asleep to speak. I am my beloved's, and his desire is toward me. Come, my beloved, let us go forth into the field; let us lodge in the villages. Let us get up early to the vineyards; let us see if the vine flourish, whether the tender grape appear, and the pomegranates bud forth: there will I give thee my love.*

The mandrakes give a smell, and at our gates are all manner of pleasant fruits, new and old, which I have laid up for thee, O my beloved. O that thou wert as my brother, that sucked the breasts of my mother! when I should find thee without, I would kiss thee; yea, I should not be despised. I would lead thee, and bring thee into my mother's house, who would instruct me: I would cause thee to drink of spiced wine of the juice of my pomegranate. His left hand should be under my head, and his right hand should embrace me. I charge you, O daughters of Jerusalem, that ye stir not up, nor awake my love, until he pleased. Who is this that cometh up from the wilderness, leaning upon her beloved? I raised thee up under the apple tree: there thy mother brought thee forth: there she brought thee forth that bare thee. Set me as a seal upon thine heart, as a seal upon thine arm: for love is strong as death; jealousy is cruel as the grave: the coals thereof are coals of fire, which hath a most vehement flame. Many waters cannot quench love, neither can the floods drown it: if a man would give all the substance of his house for love, it would be utterly contemned. We have a little sister, and she hath no breasts: what shall we do for our sister in the day when she shall be spoken for? If she be a wall, we will build upon her a palace of silver: and if she be a door, we will inclose her with boards of cedar.

I am a wall, and my breasts like towers; then was I in his eyes as one that found favour. Solomon had a vineyard at Baal-hamon; he let out the vineyard unto keepers; everyone for the fruit thereof was to bring a thousand pieces of silver. My vineyard, which is mine, is before me: thou, O Solomon, must have a thousand, and those that keep the fruit thereof two hundred. Thou that dwellest in the gardens, the companions hearken to thy voice: cause me to hear

it. Make hast, my beloved, and be thou like to a roe or to a young hart upon the mountain of spices."
Song of Solomon 1-8

10

Marry Your Soul Mate

"For this cause shall a man leave father and mother, and shall cleave to his wife: and they twain shall be one flesh? Wherefore they are no more twain, but one flesh. What therefore God hath joined together, let not man put asunder."
Matthew 19:5-6

Now that you've found your Soul Mate and quality time has been invested in the relationship there is nothing else to do but to marry the love of your life. Many times individuals want to put a lengthy time limit on when two people should marry. Who can with all certainty say that dating a person for two years or longer will guarantee a long blissful marriage without a divorce? Nor can one say with all certainty that dating a person for 6 months and then marrying them will guarantee an early divorce

In our counsel we advise others to give the relationship at least a year; this is plenty of time to see the good and bad of each other. However, it's not about time as much as it is about having sought the Lord in prayer and having a witness and peace in your spirit, having compatibility with each other and following the things you've learned in this book and other Christian books on relationships. In this book we have given you the pertinent information that's essential for finding your Soul Mate. In conclusion here is the amazing Soul Mate Course that consists of both the Chart and the Stairway to Soul Mate Land.

The Soul Mate Course Defined

1. **Stranger** = This is your starting point in your endeavor to find or be found of your soul mate. The person that you come into contact with is first off a stranger to you; this is an unknown person that you come into contact with. You may come into contact with this person in a variety of ways, to numerous to name all of the ways in detail but we will name a few. You may come in contact with this person by way of:

   - Going to the grocery store.
   - Online dating.
   - At Church.
   - At a meeting.
   - On the job.

- By introduction of someone else.
- And many other ways.

In the beginning this person is a stranger to you an unknown person that you don't know.

2. **Acquaintance =** The next circle represents someone that you want to get to know. That stranger becomes someone that you want to spend time with to get to know about. Through **time** this will become someone that you know slightly. The key here is that this person moves from being a stranger to becoming an acquaintance through the **process of time**. It doesn't happen overnight but it happens as you **spend time** to get to know the person. A legitimate question is could it happen quickly? Absolutely, but if you're not sure the process of time will answer it for you and give you the assurance and witness that you need. You may have to go through the whole chart to know, but that's okay at least you will have the assurance without a doubt that you have made the right decision and married your soul mate and not just another date.

3. **Date** = After the process of time has developed and we will not put a stipulation on how long it will take for this to occur you will then move on to the next circle which represents a date. What we have omitted is the understanding of the word date and therefore we have been destroyed for our lack of knowledge. The word date is defined as a **social** or **romantic appointment.** However, we have moved swiftly to a romantic appointment and have skipped over the first phase of dating which is simply a social appointment. The social appointments come way before the romantic appointments and the social appointments are designed because we want to know this individual. It's simply a matter of wanting to know who this individual is.

4. **Dating** = This phase of the circle goes along with the dates aspects of the **Circle of Development.** Even though the word dating is not included there this is the time when you've put in many social appointments knowing the person that eventually it moves to dating or **romantic appointment.** The social appointments will let you know through time

whether or not to move it further on to romantic appointments. If the flow is good and the connections are there then you can move on to the romantic appointments. If you aren't feeling it in the social appointments then no need to move further with romantic appointments. In romantic appointments the two of you have a connection and you're really feeling each other and a bond is developing. Now when you go on a date the conversation changes from you or I to us. At this point the conversation moves from your or my future to our future together. Romantic appointments have nothing to do with sex at all *(sex is something you want to keep out of your relationship before marriage, it simply confuses everything and God forbids it with unmarried people). Acts 15:20, 29, 21:25, 1 Corinthians 6:13, 18, 7:2, 27 10:8, Ephesians 5:3, Colossians 3:5, 1 Thessalonians 5:3* Romantic appointments gives you the opportunity to be together and bond spiritually, mentally and emotionally. Romantic appointments are only for those that have come through stages one through three in order and they're now ready for this stage four. Many think they're at stage four in the beginning but it's only a fallacy.

5. **Friends** = This phase of the circle comes after you have spent time with the person in knowing the individual and much have been discussed and revealed by the both of you. This is the phase where a bond of mutual affection has been established between the two of you. This is a really serious phase and you're really feeling the individual and they're really feeling you. You know this person and they know you and the bond is so incredible, it's like you have known this person all your life and there is a spiritual and soul (mental) connection. You enjoy being in the presence of this person and the feeling is mutual.

6. **Soul Mate** = This is the final phase of the circle and you know that this is the person that you want to spend the rest of your life with. Not only do you know this person but they know you and this has become a person not that you can live with but a person that you **(figuratively speaking)** cannot live without. This is the person that you will marry and enjoy the celebration of love that can only be found when you meet your soul mate.

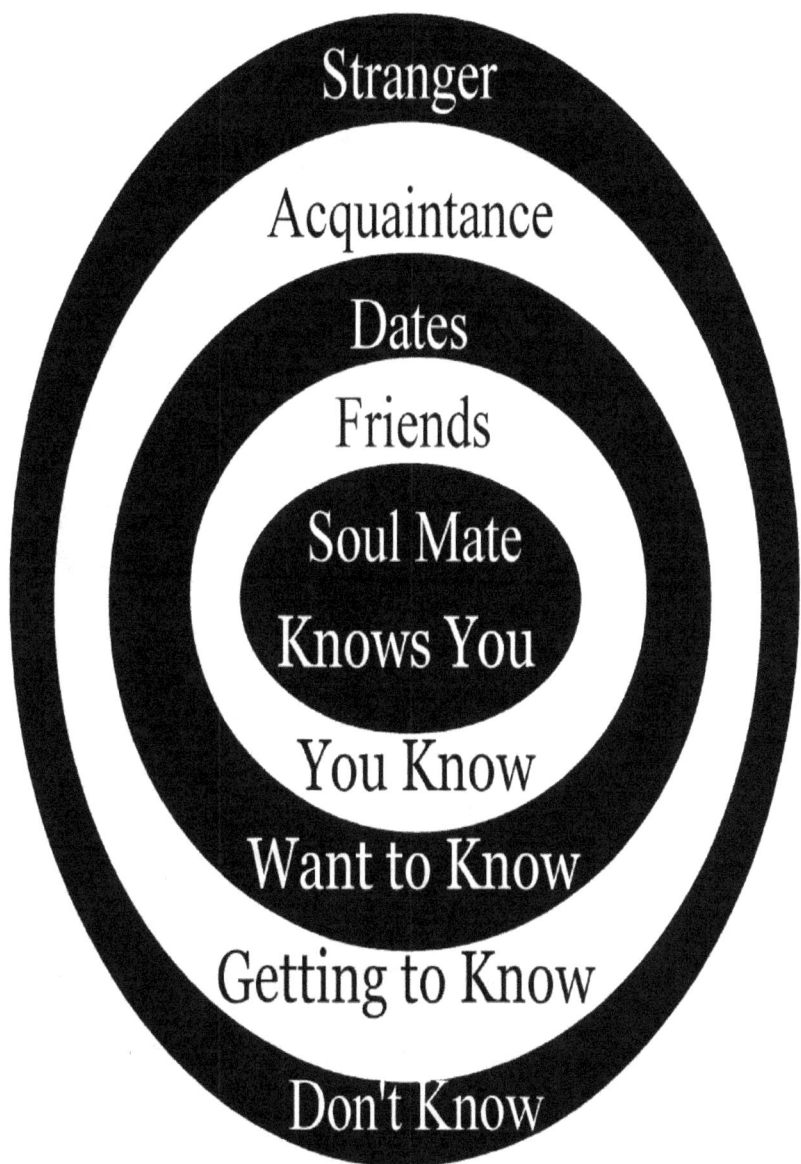

Stranger

Acquaintance

Dates

Friends

Soul Mate

Knows You

You Know

Want to Know

Getting to Know

Don't Know

Soul Mate Course

The Stairway to Soul Mate Success

Soul Mate

True love and commitment. Compatiblity and inner peace abides here.

Friend

At this stage there is a bond of mutual affection established that has come as a result of spending quality time.

Date / Dating

DATE = To have a social appointment with one another. At this stage you want to get to know one another on a more social level.

DATING = To have a romantic appointment with one another. At this stage you want to get to know one another on a more personal and intimate level.

Acquaintance

This is a person that you slightly know. This person is one step above a stranger to you. This is a person that you are getting to know and it takes time to move from here. You can't go from this step to the next overnight. Many mistakenly think so and try to rush things to the next step.

The Right Way

Just to give you an update on how things should flow from the time you begin to date a person to that blissful day of marriage the chart is a guide to show you the way. This chart will give you an understanding of how things should flow. View the chart from top to bottom to get a full understanding of the flow. We don't want you to just have an ok relationship or marriage; we want you to have a great relationship that will flow from there to a great marriage. The key to it all is getting the proper wisdom; knowledge and understanding that can enlighten your eyes so that you can see clearly and understand the right way which is God's way. The word of God says, *"Wisdom is the principal thing; therefore get wisdom: and with all thy getting get understanding." Through wisdom is an house builded; and by understanding it is established: And by knowledge shall the chambers be filled with all precious and pleasant riches." Proverbs 4:7, 24:3-4*

As the two of you include these essential elements for a blessed and fulfilling relationship the only thing that's left is to marry the person of your dreams. There are certain reasons why you want to go ahead and marry your Soul Mate and no longer put it off, reasons such as:

- You already have the witness and peace in your spirit that this is the true one.

- You may have serious passion and desires springing up in your body for one another and the Bible say, *"It's better to marry, than to burn (than have these passions and desires springing up)." 1 Corinthians 7:9*

- Your objective and desire in wanting a Soul Mate was so that you could marry. *"But and if thou marry, thou hast not sinned; and if a virgin marry, she hath not sinned." 1 Corinthians 7:28*

- Marriage is instituted and ordained by God as honorable and a good thing. *"Marriage is honourable in all, and the bed undefiled: but whoremongers and adulterers God will judge." Hebrews 13:4*

- So that the two of you can be one in the sight of God. *"For this cause shall a man leave father and mother, and shall cleave to his wife: and they twain shall be one flesh?*

Wherefore they are no more twain, but one flesh. What therefore God hath joined together, let not man put asunder." Matthew 19:5-6

- **You want to do the right thing in the sight of God and not give place to the devil to tempt you to commit fornication?**

- **Because the only next logical and reasonable step to take is to marry.**

- Sisters, when you marry the right man you will have a man that will love you even as he loves himself. Ephesians 5:33a

Don't be influenced by others that try to put a time frame on you according to what they think you should do. There are pros and cons to everything, but what it all boils down to is God and you two. It's always commendable to get counsel from those you truly respect and admire such as your Parents and your Pastor. The Bible says, *"In the multitude of counsellors there is safety." Proverbs 11:14* But don't seek the counsel of every Tom, Dick, Jane and Mary. Be led of God and seek His counsel always. You have now come to the end of your journey in knowing how to *"Let God Help You Choose Your Husband."* You now have the proper knowledge to know what it takes to know that man appointed by God for you and to marry the person of your dreams. As you go from here to marriage we will count it an honor to continue to encourage, inform and inspire you with THE SOUL MATE SERIES of books. Other books in our series are:

1. *Soul Mate or Just Another Date 2* — *Now That You've Found Your Soul Mate Here's How to Keep Them*

2. *Soul Mate or Just Another Date 3* — *For Those 50 & Over*

3. *Soul Mates In Marriage 4* — *The Love of Your Life*

4. *Soul Mates Getting Wealthy 5* — *Financial & Material Prosperity*

5. *Soul Mates In Ministry 6* — *Co-Laborers Together In the Work of The Lord.*

6. *Soul Mates Enjoying Each Other 7—* Vacation Spots, Restaurants, Outings, Hotels etc.

7. *Soul Mates Living Healthy 8—*God wants you to have long life and good health.

8. *Soul Mates Bible Study & Prayer Manuel 9—*Your Spiritual weapons to live victoriously.

9. *Kingdom Dating—*Dating for citizens of the kingdom.

10. *Kingdom Marriage—*This is the newlywed guide for citizens of the kingdom for a successful and blessed first and second year. (Also great for those that would like to improve their marriage.)

Peace and Blessings throughout Your Life!

www.ingramcontent.com/pod-product-compliance
Lightning Source LLC
Chambersburg PA
CBHW072012060426
42446CB00042B/2317